THE LEGENDS

Jonathan Bliss

Rourke Book Company, Inc.
Vero Beach, Florida 32964

The Rourke Book Co., Inc.
P.O. Box 3328, Vero Beach, FL 32964

Bliss, Jonathan.
    The legends / Jonathan Bliss.
        p.   cm. — (Hockey heroes)
    Includes bibliographical references and index.
    ISBN 1-55916-015-2
    1. Hockey players—United States—Juvenile literature. 2. Hockey players—Canada—Juvenile literature. [1. Hockey players.]
    I. Title. II. Series.
    GV848.5.A1B56   1994
    796.962'092'2—dc20
    [B]   93-42816
                                                                    CIP
                                                                     AC

Series Editor: Gregory Lee
Book design and production: The Creative Spark, San Clemente, CA
Cover photograph: Rick Stewart/ALLSPORT

Printed in the USA

Contents

*One of today's outstanding goalies and probable Hall-of-Famer:
Patrick Roy of the Montreal Canadiens.*

Great Players, Great Goalies

Hockey is such a difficult sport that it requires great skill in a number of areas to play well. First, you must be able to skate very well. Ideally, you should also skate very fast. In fact, the faster the better, since everyone else you are playing against can also skate fast.

Next, you must be able to control a puck with a curved stick. Pushing a tennis ball along the ground with a stick is hard enough, but try controlling a hard rubber disc on ice— or turning in a circle while steering the puck. How about passing the puck while racing at full speed? Now, try putting all that together without looking at the puck, paying attention to

Legends Trivia

Q: Who played the most seasons of any NHL player?
A: Gordie Howe, with 26.

Q: Who has the record for most career goals?
A: Gordie Howe, with 801.

Q: Name the goalie with the most career shutouts.
A: Terry Sawchuk, with 103.

Q: Who has scored three or more goals in a game the most times?
A: Wayne Gretzky has done it 49 times.

that 230-pound defenseman bearing down on you at 30 miles an hour.

While we're on the subject of defensemen, don't forget that you must be able to take a hit—make that many hits. Pain is definitely part of the game. Few hockey players have gotten through a career without earning some scars or losing teeth.

We still haven't gotten to the really hard part. You must be able to shoot the puck, too. Not just shoot it, but aim it so accurately that you can hit a bull's-eye with it at 30 feet. Most baseball pitchers don't have this kind of control, yet in hockey it is absolutely necessary. But the net—your target—is six feet across by four feet high. No problem, right? Wrong. There's always this large man with pads hogging the goal's mouth, and his sole purpose in life is to stop that puck at any cost.

How about stamina? Hockey, more than any other sport except long-distance running, requires endurance. In fact, the game is so taxing that most professional players can only afford to spend one or two minutes at a time on the ice. Lines are often shifted every 45 seconds to keep players fresh and allow them to catch their breath. Any player who can skate more than 20 minutes in a hockey game is a phenomenon.

Finally, there are the little things that make the difference between an average minor league hockey player and a player who reaches the big time: grace, rink sense, durability, and courage. Let's not forget swift reflexes. The game is too fast. If you want a chance to think before you make a move, pick chess. But if you like your action fast, choose hockey.

Now, all players in the National Hockey League (NHL) must be able to do the above. But how does one become a superstar of the game? Selecting hockey's greatest players is tricky. Someone is always left out. Perhaps some others are needlessly included. Let's just say that this book contains a list of some of hockey's greatest all-time players.

Netminders of the Early Years

The success of a team is usually measured by its goaltender. This is a simple fact. All the great forwards in the world cannot make up for a leaky net in your own end. Again and again throughout hockey history, the man behind the mask has been the difference between a good team and a great one. Here are some of the greatest goalies in hockey history.

Measured by any statistic, George Hainsworth was one of the greatest goalies ever. He was one big reason why the Montreal Canadiens were so hard to beat during the 1920s and early 1930s. Hainsworth didn't crack under pressure—he remained calm, a great quality in a goalie who must wait patiently to be attacked. Hainsworth turned pro in 1923 with Saskatoon and remained with that team until 1926, when he shifted to Montreal. He was an immediate sensation, being the first player to win the Vezina Trophy (and the next two years as well). His most impressive year was the 1928-29 season, when he allowed only 43 goals in 44 games! That put Hainsworth's goals-against average at 0.98—an unbelievable feat. Even more impressive: he maintained a tiny goals-against average for his career: a cool 1.91 in 465 regular-season games and 1.93 in 52 playoff games.

Frankie Brimsek replaced Hall-of-Famer Tiny Thompson in the nets for the Boston Bruins in the middle of the 1938-39 season and faced the near-impossible task of living up to Thompson's reputation. But "Mr. Zero" turned in six shutouts in his first eight starts, including a consecutive scoreless streak of 231 minutes. Brimsek was one of the first American-born All-Stars in the league, and became wildly popular in

Boston. He led the Bruins to the regular season championship and the Stanley Cup. The Bruins won two more league championships and one more Stanley Cup (1940-41) with Brimsek in the nets over the next three years. He spent four more years with Boston and another year with Chicago before retiring. He left behind him several records, two Vezina Trophies, two Stanley Cups, and a fine 2.7 regular season goals-against mark (2.58 GAA for the playoffs).

Walter "Turk" Broda's hockey career started on the day his public school principal in Brandon, Manitoba assigned him to play goalie for the school's hockey team. Despite never playing goalie before, he was a natural at it, and quickly rose through the junior ranks. Eventually, he came to the attention of Conn Smythe, owner of the Toronto Maple Leafs. Smythe was scouting for a goalie to replace Hall-of-Famer George Hainsworth. He came to see a Winsor Bulldog player named Robertson, but liked the goalie for the opposing team better. It was Turk Broda. After he replaced Hainsworth in the 1936-37 season, he held the job for 14 seasons. During their golden years the Maple Leafs enjoyed Broda's awesome 302 wins, 224 losses, and 101 ties for a 2.53 GAA. The Leafs were the first NHL franchise to win three Stanley Cups in a row, and four Cups in five years. Part of the reason for that record was certainly Broda. Broda's goals-against average during playoff games was just 1.98.

Success doesn't always come overnight. Take the case of Bill Durnan. He was 29 years old before he got his chance at the major league level. One of his problems was the organization he was in: The Montreal Canadiens was a tough team to find a place on, particularly for a goalie, because you were always replacing an All-Star. The Canadiens finally brought up

Durnan in 1943, and he made an immediate impression. He was big, quick, and had tremendous desire. In his brief hockey career, Durnan won the Vezina Trophy six times in seven years. During the 1948-49 season he set the league's modern record for longest shutout sequence when he held his opponents scoreless for 309 minutes! He

Turk Broda was the secret to the Toronto Maple Leafs' success during the 1930s.

credited much of his success to a former coach who had taught him how to switch his stick from one hand to another. He had so many stickhandling skills that he often acted like a third defenseman in his own end.

Goalies of the 1950s and '60s

Glenn Hall was the first great goalie of the modern era. Hall claimed to be a bundle of nerves before every game, claiming the job of goalie was "torture," but you could never tell that by his play. He fought "between the pipes" with the best, and became an immediate success with the Detroit Red Wings. He won the Calder Trophy as the NHL's top rookie in 1956, and with his 12 shutouts helped the Red Wings to win their fourth Stanley Cup in six years. Hall played a record 502 consecutive games. After two years with Detroit, Hall spent a decade playing for the Chicago Black Hawks,

With each passing decade, the Montreal Canadiens continued to hire one hockey superstar after another, including Jacques Plante.

winning the Vezina Trophy three times as the league's outstanding goalie. He was named to the All-Star first team five times. He reached the peak of his career in 1961 when the Black Hawks won the Stanley Cup for the first time in 23 years. During the semifinals against Montreal, Hall held back the monster offense of Hall-of-Famers Jean Beliveau, Bernie "Boom Boom" Geoffrion, Dickie Moore, and Henri Richard, leaving them scoreless for 135 minutes. Hall was inducted into the Hall of Fame in 1975.

Jacques Plante's career began with a bang. His first game with the Montreal Canadiens was a Stanley Cup playoff game at Chicago. He was so nervous he couldn't tie his skates, but he still shut out the

Black Hawks 3-0. Plante spent 10 years with the Canadiens, helping them to five straight Stanley Cup championships (1956 through 1960). He won the Vezina Trophy a record-tying six times. Plante was an agile goalie, originating a style of play that was new: He went roving beyond the crease to intercept oncoming players before they could get off a shot, cutting down the angle on a shot whenever possible, sometimes becoming a third defenseman on the ice.

The goalie behind the Edmonton Oilers' dynasty of the 1980s was Grant Fuhr—one of the NHL's first black superstars.

After a brief retirement, Plante came back in 1968 to play for a while with the St. Louis Blues, sharing the net with another star, 37-year-old Glenn Hall. Together they shared a Vezina Trophy while leading the Blues to two consecutive Western Division titles. Plante's lifetime goals-against average was 2.38, with 82 shutouts (for a 434-246-137 mark). Plante joined the other greats in the Hall of Fame in 1978.

Gump Worsley was an unlikely hockey star. He was shorter and broader than most NHL players. However, that shape made him fit nicely in the crease. He was far quicker than he looked, and his fearlessness (he didn't wear a mask) was legendary. Worsley was the anchor of the New York Rangers' defense—in fact, he was very nearly the only defense for that hobbled team during the 1950s. Gump averaged less than three goals-against per game, almost single-handedly keeping the Rangers in games.

In 1963, Worsley was given a chance to play for the defense-minded Montreal Canadiens. Soon more fans came to appreciate his talent, because his GAA dropped from 3.0 to 1.98. Worsley was nearly 35 when he finally won a Stanley Cup with the Canadiens in 1965, shutting out the Chicago Black Hawks, 4-0, in the final game of the series. He would enjoy four more Cup championships before ending his career with the Minnesota North Stars in 1974. He finally wore a mask in this, his 24th season!

The Shutout King

During the course of his 21 years in the NHL trenches (1949-70), Terry Sawchuk sustained at least six injuries that would have ended the careers of lesser players, but he fought back each time. He is a model of courage. One of his most serious injuries was losing sight in his right eye. Despite this and many other hardships, Terry Sawchuk emerged as one of the best goalies ever.

Sawchuk broke into professional hockey as a netminder for Omaha of the United States Hockey League. He won the league's rookie of the year award and spent the next two years in the American Hockey League. Then, in 1950, Terry joined the Detroit Red Wings. Though he looked slow and cumbersome, he moved with great speed, and his fierce style became popular with fans. In his first full year in the league he recorded an amazing 1.99 GAA with 11 shutouts, earning the first of four Vezina Trophies.

Sawchuk also played for Boston, Toronto, Los Angeles, and New York, establishing a career GAA of 2.5 with 115 shutouts, making him the only NHL goalie to record more than 100 in a career.

Ken Dryden

Ken Dryden was one imposing goalie. With his six-feet, four-inch, 205-pound frame, Dryden seemed to take up the whole net. But he wasn't just a great athlete. Dryden was just as comfortable in the classroom as he was in the crease, working his way through Cornell University on a partial hockey scholarship. He became a lawyer while earning money playing in the NHL.

Phil Esposito, the premier puck handler of Dryden's generation, once called Dryden "an octopus." He meant that Dryden could find the puck anywhere, reach out and grab it to protect his net. Dryden debuted with the Canadiens in 1970, allowing only nine goals in his first six games. His team won the Stanley Cup that year, and Dryden took the Conn Smythe Trophy as the playoff MVP. In 1971, his first full year in the NHL, he won the Calder Trophy as the rookie of the year. There's only one word for Dryden's reign: dominating. In seven-plus seasons for the Canadiens, he played every playoff game, and his team won four straight Stanley Cups as a result (from 1975 to 1979). He was named to the NHL All-Star team five times, led the league in shutouts four times, and won the Vezina Trophy five times. In short, Dryden might lose a game, but rarely two in a row. Dryden was simply unbeatable.

When he retired in 1979, Dryden had a remarkable 2.24 regular-season GAA including 46 shutouts (resulting in an unprecedented 258-57-74 record).

*Defense is the overlooked side of hockey; often, tough competitors
collide for control of the puck.*

Defense Is Their Game

Traditionally, defensemen are the tough guys on the team. They serve as the front line of defense for the goalie and the back line for the forwards. They are also the middlemen of hockey, usually last in the adoration of fans, caught between the glamorous goal-scoring forwards and the spectacular goal-saving goalies. Yet few teams have ever been able to climb out of the basement without them. Neither a great goalie nor an All-Star forward can compensate for shoddy defense.

Hockey purists believe Eddie Shore was the greatest defenseman ever. His brand of hockey was simple: He defended his zone no matter what. If that meant clobbering a few forwards and getting into fights, that was just fine by Shore. He liked it that way. During his career (1926 to 1940) with the Boston Bruins, Shore was known as the meanest defenseman in the league. He was part of two Stanley Cup-winning teams. But he was more than just a defensive weapon. He was a real crowd-pleaser, and when he had the puck the crowds responded enthusiastically, because things always happened when Shore was in control. He was a playmaker. Shore is the only defenseman ever to win the Hart Trophy for the league's Most Valuable Player four times (1933, 1935, 1936, and 1938), and he was voted to the All-Star team eight times.

The Gentleman of Defense

Patrick "Red" Kelly was one of the best and most versatile athletes in hockey. During his years in the NHL he played defenseman, center, and wing. But he broke into the league in 1947 as a defenseman, and it is at this position that he is usually remembered. In his 12 years with the Detroit Red Wings, he established himself as the best rushing defenseman in the league. Agile and quick, he presented one more threat to the opposing team that was already faced with the famous "Production Line" of Ted Lindsay, Sid Abel, and Gordie Howe. Although Kelly was a deft passer and an excellent playmaker, he was no bruiser. Not many defensemen are awarded the Lady Byng Trophy (not once but four times) for sportsmanlike play. Kelly relied on superior size and speed rather than slamming players. With Kelly on defense, Detroit won eight regular season championships and four Stanley Cup titles. Kelly was also the first recipient of the Norris Trophy (1954) for the league's outstanding defenseman.

Defensive Domination

Doug Harvey was such a tough defenseman that he monopolized the Norris Trophy, winning it a record seven times between 1955 and 1962. A left-handed shot, Harvey was an excellent blocker and had uncanny puck control. The Montreal Canadiens counted on him to control the pace of the game. With his remarkable skating and stickhandling, Harvey did. If they needed to kill time, Harvey brought the puck up-ice slowly. If Montreal needed a quick score, Harvey could usually get it for them by winding up in his own end, then charging down the ice, passing off to one of his forwards or shooting the puck himself.

Harvey led the Canadiens to five straight Stanley Cup championships from 1956 to 1960. During his 13 seasons with Montreal, he was named to the All-Star team 10 times. More of a playmaker than a scorer, Harvey never scored more than eight goals in a season, but he accumulated 452 assists.

The amazing Bobby Orr was regarded as the greatest athlete of his era.

The Age of Orr

When it comes to naming the greatest defenseman in NHL history, there can only be one answer: Bobby Orr. No one had greater natural gifts or a better work ethic than Orr. Here was a muscular and speedy skater, one with an uncanny sense for playing the game. He was the most formidable player of his era at any position.

Orr changed the traditional role of the defenseman all by himself. Prior to his appearance, most defensemen stayed back, protecting their own zone, participating little in up-ice rushes. Scoring was not their job. Orr changed all that. He was so gifted that he could ignore the rules. Faster than any other player in the sport, Orr became known for his end-to-end rushes. They were dramatic, breathtaking things. Orr could avoid any opponent simply by outskating him. He could keep the puck away from anyone who tried to poke it away. He had a cannon for a slapshot, a wicked wristshot, and could thread the puck past a goalie no matter how small the opening.

Orr did not neglect his defensive duties. He could steal the puck better than almost anyone, he could bodycheck with the best in the league, and, when called on, he wasn't afraid of a fight. He was also an outstanding penalty killer.

Orr signed a record two-year contract with the Boston Bruins at the age of 19. In his first year (1967) Orr won the Calder Trophy as the top rookie. His coach, Harry Sinden, said, "Bobby was a star from the moment they played the National Anthem in his first NHL game." Orr won the Norris Trophy eight straight years, and in 1970 he became the first man in NHL history to win four trophies in a single season: the Norris Trophy, the Art Ross Trophy for the top scoring title, the Hart Trophy as the league's MVP, and the Conn Smythe Trophy as the playoff MVP. Did the Bruins win the Stanley Cup that year? Of course.

Before Orr, no defenseman had ever won the scoring championship. Orr did it with ease; he had 33 goals and 87 assists for 120 points. A defenseman scoring more than 100 points was unheard of. The following year, Orr did himself one better, scoring a blistering 139 points. Only teammate Phil Esposito outpointed him with 152 points. The following season, Esposito and Orr were again numbers one and two in league scoring. Orr won the Hart Trophy for the third straight year.

Orr's career-best was 46 goals during the 1974-75 season. He was also named to the All-Star team for the eighth consecutive year. Boston hoped Orr would never grow old, but Orr had bad knees. On November 1, 1978, Bobby Orr retired. He was only 30 years old. Despite a little over 11 seasons in the NHL, Orr held or shared 12 individual records. He was voted into the Hockey Hall of Fame in 1979.

Denis Potvin

When 19-year-old Denis Potvin appeared in the New York Islanders training camp in 1973, he was met with great expectations. He had already smashed Bobby Orr's Ontario Hockey League records for a defenseman. Potvin never claimed to be as great a skater as Orr, but he was a ferocious hitter. His physical style of play earned him the respect of many players in the NHL, and his excellent passing made him the playmaker the Islanders needed.

Potvin won the Calder Trophy as the NHL's Rookie of the Year. In the next 14 seasons, Potvin won the Norris Trophy three times, and was a first-team All-Star five times. He also captained the New York Islanders during their four-year domination of the Stanley Cup from 1980 through 1983. When he retired in 1988, Potvin had broken three of Orr's greatest records for a defenseman: most goals (310), most assists (742), and most career points (1,052).

A Durable Player

He was just a farm kid born near Ottawa, but Larry Robinson gained fame as one of the NHL's finest defenseman. He was really the prototype for the modern defenseman: a fast skater with a strong physique who played well enough to be a forward (a position he occasionally played). Brought up by the Canadiens during the 1972-73 season, Robinson became the team's mainstay for 16 seasons. His greatest offensive season came in 1976-77 when he scored 19 goals and 85 assists, won the Norris Trophy, and was named to the All-Star team. A year later, he won the Conn Smythe Trophy as the playoff MVP in the playoffs, scoring four goals and 17 assists in 15 games as Montreal won their first of four straight Stanley Cups.

The durable Larry Robinson (19) outlasted many other players to become one of the great defensemen in hockey history.

An outstanding blocker and checker, Robinson's forte was strategy and positioning. He always seemed to set up exactly where the offense wanted to go and had an uncanny sense for the puck. He triggered the offense as well as anyone in the league with an assortment of soft passes and a menacing slapshot from the point on power plays.

Robinson played with the Los Angeles Kings from 1989 to 1992, and earned his eighth appearance in an

All-Star game. When he retired, he had 208 career goals and 750 assists in 1,384 games (ninth on the all-time NHL games played list).

More Bruin Power

Not since Orr has a defenseman excited the Boston fans like Ray Bourque. Bourque's style isn't nearly so fast and flashy, but still there are similarities. In his first NHL game, Bourque scored a goal and two assists. He won the Calder Trophy for the league's best rookie, and he was selected to the All-Star team—the only non-goalie ever to win both honors in a single year. From that point on, Bourque never missed an All-Star game.

Bourque's endurance is one of his secrets. He frequently logs between 35 and 40 minutes a game. In addition to his stamina, Bourque is also strong, able to keep opponents away from his net. Bourque has always been up near the top of the Plus/Minus stats (goals-for versus goals-against while the player is on the ice), one of the more dependable indications of a defenseman's prowess.

Bourque's other asset is his offensive skills. He seems to know just the right moment to stuff the puck into the net. Not that Bourque always looks to score. Bourque had his best offensive year in 1983-84, when he tallied 31 goals and 65 assists for 96 points. He has won four Norris Trophies. At last count, he had accumulated more than 300 goals and 780 assists in more than 1,000 games. Few players today are more likely to enter the Hall of Fame than Ray Bourque.

Oily Competitor

On the ice, Paul Coffey is terribly fast and offensive-minded. Coffey is the only other defenseman besides Orr to challenge the NHL scoring lead. When he was drafted in 1980 by the Edmonton Oilers, Coffey

Paul Coffey (left) became the "new" Bobby Orr when he passed Orr's record of most goals in a season by a defenseman.

joined Wayne Gretzky, Mark Messier, Grant Fuhr, Jari Kurri, and Glenn Anderson to form one of the greatest hockey teams of all time.

In the 1982-83 season, Coffey accumulated an incredible 126 points to become the second-leading scorer in the NHL. He won his third invitation to the All-Star game, and helped Edmonton win their first of five Stanley Cups.

Coffey had his best offensive year in 1985-86, when he scored 48 goals, snapping Bobby Orr's once untouchable record of 46 goals. He ended the season with 138 points—third overall in the NHL behind Gretzky and Mario Lemieux—amazing for any defenseman (and only one point shy of Orr's all-time record for defensemen). Eight of Coffey's points came on March 14, 1986 when he tied the NHL mark for defensemen and equaled the defensemen's record for assists in one game with six. Coffey was even more devastating in the playoffs as he scored 12 goals and 25 assists in 18 games (both are NHL records for defensemen).

Coffey was traded before the start of the 1987-88 season to Pittsburgh. But he didn't miss out on the Stanley Cup competition, because the Penguins were the up-and-coming team. Coffey still had someone to pass to: Instead of center Wayne Gretzky, it was now Mario Lemieux. Then in 1991, he was traded in quick succession to the Kings and then to the Red Wings. In 14 NHL seasons, Coffey has accumulated more than 330 goals, 800 assists, and 1,100 points—all career records for a defenseman. He also holds the record for most goals, assists, and points by a defenseman in the playoffs.

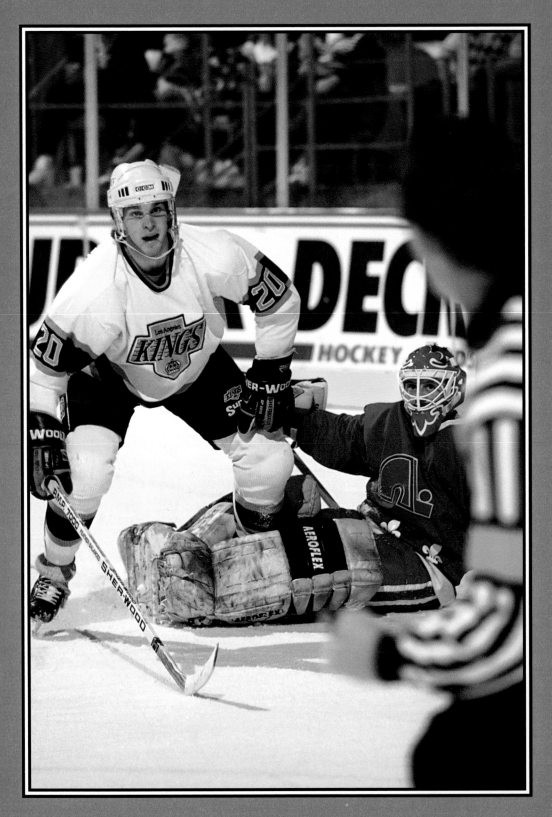

One of today's top forwards is Luc Robitaille.

Wingers on the Attack

The right and left wingers are two-thirds of a hockey team's forward line offense. They are expected to score while the goalie and the defensemen concentrate on preventing goals. The wingers' success is measured by point totals, and those who produce become good hockey players. The list of truly great wingers is found in the Hall of Fame. The few mentioned here are generally considered to be the best of the best.

During his great career, Maurice "Rocket" Richard collected more offensive records than anyone in the league. In his day, Richard was certainly the greatest winger.

Detroit's Ted Lindsay was one-third of the great Red Wing "Production Line" which included Gordie Howe.

Richard joined the Canadiens in 1942-43 after several sparkling seasons in both junior and senior leagues. In his first 16 games, he scored five goals. On the ice, he was a runner, not a glider, so his style wasn't graceful, but it was effective. Richard outhustled everyone else.

Richard was physically strong, bowling over any defenseman in his path. He could put the puck and a defenseman into the opposing goal! Richard also had a mean temper and got into frequent scrapes with opposing players and referees. But perhaps Richard's greatest ability was his native talent for the game. Like many of the truly great players, his immense talent was based on instinct. Canadien General Manager Frank Selke said Richard was "the greatest opportunist the game has ever known."

Richard was the third member of the Canadiens' high-scoring Punch Line (including Toe Blake at left wing, and Elmer Lach at center). Their first year together, the line scored 86 goals; 32 belonged to the Rocket. Then, during the second game of the playoffs, the Rocket scored all five of Montreal's goals.

During the 1944-45 season, Richard streaked through the 50-game schedule at an incredible one goal-per-game clip, including 15 goals in one nine-game stretch. Richard was the first player ever to score 50 goals in a season.

Richard has so many records to his credit that they can't all be listed here. He helped guide the Canadiens to eight Stanley Cups while compiling an impressive career mark of 544 goals in 978 games. When Richard finally hung up his skates in 1960, the NHL inducted the Rocket into the Hall of Fame without the customary waiting period.

Red Wing Fury

Most of Ted Lindsay's opponents were taller and heavier, but none were as tough or talented. This left winger wore the scars of his NHL battles with pride (more than 400 stitches worth). Despite the scar tissue, Lindsay was beautiful to watch on the ice. He joined the Detroit Red Wings in 1944 at the age of 19. He played with right wing Gordie Howe and center Sid Abel, forming the legendary "Production Line." Lindsay and his offensive linemates led the Red Wings to eight regular season league titles (including seven in a row) and four Stanley Cup championships between 1949 and 1955.

Lindsay had a string of great offensive years with the Red Wings, but perhaps his best was 1949-50 when he led the league in scoring with 78 points (23 goals and 55 assists). Sid Abel and Gordie Howe finished second and third. Lindsay saved his greatest heroics for the playoff finals. The Red Wings were behind 3-2 in the series. When his team was down by one goal to the Rangers, Lindsay tied the score with minutes to play in the third period. Sid Abel came through with the clincher, and Detroit went on to defeat New York 4-3 for the Stanley Cup.

Lindsay played 16 seasons and then retired—or so everyone thought. Four years later, at age 39, he came back. Using his trademark brawling style, Lindsay helped the Red Wings finish in first place for the first time in eight years. It was one of the most remarkable comebacks in professional sports.

Ted Lindsay's partner on right wing was and is a legend. Gordie Howe is hockey's most enduring spirit. Along with Wayne Gretzky and Bobby Orr, Howe must certainly be considered one of the greatest in hockey history. Jean Beliveau, one of Howe's fiercest rivals, said, "Gordie Howe is the best hockey player I have ever seen."

Like many legends, Howe combined so many fine skills that it is hard to single out any one of his talents. He was a graceful skater. When he had the puck, it was glued to his stick. He could haul the puck in and shoot it in one, fluid motion. He was strong, and could shoot with equal authority from either side of the rink. He could thread a puck through the eye of a needle, if necessary. And Howe withstood three decades of pounding without any apparent sign of wear.

He joined the Detroit Red Wings for the 1946-47 season when he was 18 years old, and the Red Wings first assembled the Production Line of Sid Abel (center), Ted Lindsay (left wing) and Howe (right wing). By 1950, their attack became a juggernaut that would dominate hockey for five years. Detroit finished first in the regular season for an unprecedented seven straight years. More impressive, Howe and the Red Wings would capture four Stanley Cups in six years.

Howe was a fixture at the top of the hockey world throughout the 1950s and much of the '60s. Howe broke the all-time record for career goals when he passed Maurice Richard's mark of 544 goals. Howe made 21 appearances in the All-Star game, and retired at age 51! Howe left records too numerous to list, and a few that will probably stand forever, including most NHL seasons (26) and most NHL games played (1,767).

The Golden Jet

Bobby Hull had two talents that, when combined, were positively frightening. He had the strongest slapshot in hockey, and he was the league's fastest skater in his day. Imagine a speed demon on the ice launching a 100-mph shot at your goal, and you have the threat that was Bobby Hull. But Hull's slapshot wasn't wild and out of control; it was accurate. Hull averaged 40 goals each year during 16 seasons.

"The Golden Jet" became a star in Chicago, where he became the first player to score more than 50 goals in a season (1961-62), slamming 54 home. By 1968-69, Hull had increased that mark to 58 goals in a season. He played left wing on 10 All-Star teams. He won the Hart Trophy for MVP twice, and the Lady Byng sportsmanship trophy once. He became the league's highest-paid player in 1968, and led the Black Hawks to a Stanley Cup. Bobby Hull was the franchise. When he

The swiftest skater of the 1960s and '70s—Bobby Hull—also had a mean slapshot.

retired in 1980, Hull was the highest-scoring left wing in history, with 1,018 goals and 2,017 assists. In 119 playoff games, Hull scored 62 goals and 67 assists.

Stars of the 1970s

Guy Lafleur was another in a long line of great Montreal Canadien stars. From Howie Morenz and the Brothers Richard to Jean Beliveau, Lafleur was a cut above. He had superior speed; a hard, accurate shot; and great stickhandling. The right winger was also creative; the normal rush up-ice was not enough for him. He improvised, passing behind his back to a teammate, or passing the puck to himself through the opposing player's legs. It was exciting to see what Lafleur would do next.

From 1974 to 1980, Lafleur had 50-plus goal seasons. He was the consistent All-Star selection at right wing, and won the Art Ross Trophy as scoring champ three times. He was league MVP twice. And he was there to push the Canadiens to four consecutive Stanley Cups. Lafleur was traded to the New York Rangers in 1980 and then to Quebec a year later. When he finally retired in 1985, he had compiled 518 goals and 728 assists in 961 career games.

Mike Bossy did it more times than anyone could remember, that is, he made magic shots on goal. Now you see it, now you don't. His stick was a blur, and suddenly the puck was past the goalie and in the net. Mike Bossy was a pure shooter. Unlike most other superstars, Bossy's entrance into the league was not preceded by much fanfare. He entered the league quietly, selected 15th overall in the 1977 draft by the New York Islanders. But by the end of his first year, people were talking plenty about him. Bossy scored a record 53 goals and won the Calder Trophy as the league's best rookie. For the next nine seasons, Bossy would score 50 goals or better—in five of them scoring 60 or better! No one had ever come close to such totals; not Hull, not Howe, not Richard. Bossy was forced to retire in 1988 because of a chronic bad back. He was only 31. Despite a comparatively short NHL career, Bossy left behind him an impressive record of accomplishment, with 573 goals and 553 assists in only 752 games—an average of more than one point per game.

A New Generation

Brett Hull is the son of the legendary Bobby Hull. The Golden Jet of the 1960s begat The Golden Brett of

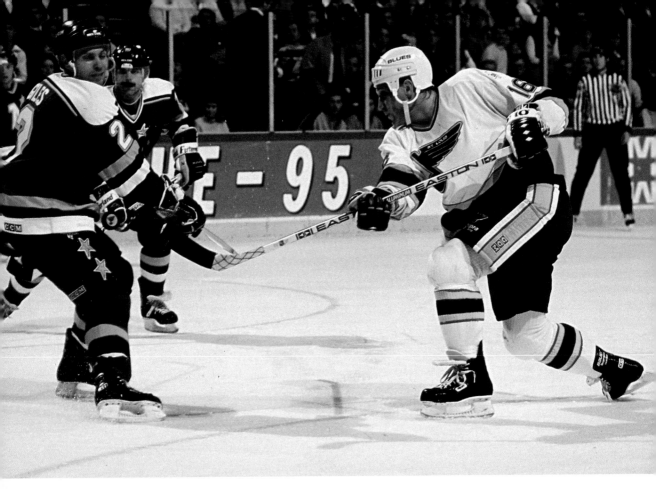

Don't look now, but that's the son of Bobby Hull, Brett, making his own way into the hockey superstar ranks.

the 1990s. Brett Hull plays right wing instead of left wing, but the slapshot looks familiar: a blinding blur of rubber that reaches nearly 130 m.p.h. If anything, Hull is an even better skater than his father, holding his own against a throng of defenders.

After playing briefly with the Calgary Flames, Hull moved to the St. Louis Blues where he became a star. In 1988-89, he scored 41 goals and 43 assists, and St. Louis was in second place in the Norris Division. The following year, Hull set the right wing record for most goals in a season (72), breaking Jarri Kurri's mark of 71. Hull shattered all the records the next year, scoring 86 goals and 45 assists. Only Wayne Gretzky had ever scored that many goals before. The fact is, Hull is running out of mantle space for his many trophies.

His name means "the Flower": Guy Lafleur played sensational wing for the Canadiens, Rangers, and Nordiques.

*Wayne Gretzky will enter the Hall of Fame with more records and
honors than any other hockey player in history.*

Center Stage

Like the quarterback in football, the center is responsible for taking the face-offs, for setting up the play, and for scoring the goals. While he is occasionally overshadowed by talented wingers, most of the time the centerman is in the middle of the action. He must be a good passer and a good scorer. Because of his position on the ice, it is no wonder that the highest-profile players of today—and many of the most prolific scorers from the past—were centermen. Here are a few of the finest centers who have ever played the game.

Joe Malone was one of the first great goal scorers. During his 15-year career (1909-24), Malone was credited with 379 goals—most gained in only seven seasons. He was a star in the National Hockey Association before playing in the

---

Legends Trivia

Q: Who holds the record for the most points scored in one period?
A: Bryan Trottier (Islanders), on December 23, 1978 against the the New York Rangers.

Q: Who holds the record for the most wins by a goalie in one season?
A: Bernie Parent (Philadelphia), with 47, in 1973-74.

Q: Who holds the record for the fastest three goals?
A: Bill Mosienko (Chicago), who scored a hat trick in 21 seconds against the Rangers on March 23, 1952.

NHL, scoring 41 goals in 20 games during one remarkable season. Some of his legendary single-game performances included an amazing nine goals against the Sydney Millionaires in a 1913 Stanley Cup playoff game; eight against the Montreal Wanderers in 1917; and seven against Toronto in 1920—a mark that still stands as an NHL single-game record.

During the 1920s and '30s, Howie Morenz was the Babe Ruth of hockey. He attracted attention early in his career when he scored nine goals in an amateur game in 1922. They dubbed him "The Stratford Streak" because of his quickness, but Morenz never skated away from a bodycheck despite his relatively small 165-pound frame. In 1928, he won the Hart Trophy as the best player in the NHL after collecting 33 goals and 18 assists in only 43 games. He led the Canadiens to two consecutive Stanley Cups (1929-30 and 1939-31), scoring an astounding 40 goals and 10 assists in 44 games. Toe Blake, the most successful coach in Montreal history, said of Morenz: "He was an inspiration for all of us...a man with remarkable skills who laughed hard and played hard." In 1950, Howie Morenz was the runaway winner in a Canadian Press poll as the outstanding hockey player of the first half century.

A Boston Star

Milt Schmidt played center on one of the most potent offensive lines in NHL history. With Woody Dumart and Bobby Bauer at wings, Schmidt and company led the Bruins to four straight regular-season NHL championships and two Stanley Cups. He was known as a hard hitter, and never gave up the puck without a fight. He was also a great passer, leading some to claim that Schmidt was the fastest playmaker of all time. He always seemed to know where everyone else was on the ice and could maneuver the puck and his

One of the most exciting centers in Canadiens' history was the man who anchored their 10 Stanley Cup-run: Jean Beliveau.

linemates into just the right position for a score. Schmidt would also play hurt, earning the respect of opposing players and even referees. During his NHL career he scored 229 goals and 346 assists for a total of 575 points.

Jean Beliveau

The Montreal Canadiens had to buy an entire hockey league just to get Jean Beliveau. It was a wise investment. In 1953, Beliveau was in his third season in the Quebec Senior League. When the Canadiens couldn't lure Beliveau away from that league, they bought it! They acquired the rights to everybody, and Beliveau finally signed a big contract.

He entered the NHL in 1953 as the most exciting rookie of the decade. Beliveau scored 37 goals and 36 assists in his first year—nearly as many as teammates Bernie Geoffrion and Maurice Richard. He narrowly missed out on his first Stanley Cup victory when Detroit's Alex Delvecchio scored two goals in the seventh game of the finals to beat Montreal.

In 1955-56 Beliveau scored a league-best 47 goals and 41 assists, and the Canadiens won the Stanley Cup. To cap the season, Beliveau also collected the Hart Trophy as the league's best player. Although he was big and immovable when he had the puck, he avoided fights. Beliveau's leadership helped make the Canadiens nearly unbeatable. Through the 1950s and '60s they boasted one of the finest teams of all time. Beliveau captained them through 10 Stanley Cups. In his final year (1970-71), Beliveau collected 16 playoff assists and his tenth Stanley Cup triumph.

Stan Mikita

Stan Mikita entered the NHL in 1958-59 with the Chicago Black Hawks, and embarked on a brilliant career that spanned 20 full seasons. Mikita was a natural team leader, and Chicago won the Stanley Cup for the first time in decades in only his third year as a player. Mikita's scoring and passing prowess became so dependable that he routinely earned between 50 and 60 assists a season.

In 1966-67, Mikita became the first player to win the Ross, Hart, and Lady Byng trophies for top scorer, MVP, and sportsmanlike play in the same season. When Mikita retired from hockey in 1980, he had played in

1,394 games over 20 seasons with the same club, and had scored 541 goals and 926 assists.

Phil Esposito

Few players have better career starts than Phil Esposito. He played center for the Chicago Black Hawks alongside superstar winger Bobby Hull, scoring 71 goals in three seasons with the club. But that wasn't enough for Chicago, who traded him to the Boston Bruins—a big mistake. In eight-plus years with Boston, Esposito won five scoring championships. He was the first man in hockey history to score more than 100 points in a season, and surpassed the 50-goal mark five times! With his help, the Bruins walked away with the Stanley Cup handily after 29 years of waiting. In 1972-73, Esposito and the Bruins won another Stanley Cup.

Esposito was the consummate center. He rarely moved from in front of the net because he was too strong to be moved. His wristshot was a nightmare to opposing goalies. For his career, Esposito played in 1,282 games spanning 18 NHL seasons. He scored a total of 1,590 points on 717 goals and 873 assists. Only Gordie Howe had more goals (801) and more points (1,850) than Esposito—but Howe had attained those totals over the course of many more games.

Islander Star

Few players in modern history have been better at winning than Bryan Trottier. Trottier in his prime may have been as great as Wayne Gretzky. One of the greatest players, Gordie Howe, thought so. Trottier became a New York Islander in 1975. In his second game, he scored three goals and equaled a club single-game record with five points. He walked away with the Calder Trophy as the league's best rookie, setting two league records for a rookie: most assists (63) and most points (95).

Many fans have compared the play of Byran Trottier with that of Wayne Gretzky. He is fifth on the all-time list for career assists.

With Trottier's help, the Islanders proceeded to win four straight Stanley Cups beginning in 1980. Together with linemate Mike Bossy, this duo formed one of the most lethal scoring combinations in league history. "It was eerie at times," said Trottier of his playing relationship with Bossy, "I would start a sentence and Mike would finish it. We always knew what the other was thinking."

Trottier's career seemed over when he was released by the Islanders in 1990. But Trottier immediately signed as a free agent with the Pittsburgh

Mark Messier has had an outstanding career with both the Edmonton Oilers of the 1980s and the Rangers in the '90s.

Penguins, and suddenly found himself playing on the same team with Mario Lemieux. They won back-to-back Stanley Cups in 1991 and 1992! To date, Trottier has played in eight All-Star games and holds or shares many records, including most points in a period (6) and most goals in a period (4).

Mark Messier

During the 1980s, the Edmonton Oilers had an enviable combination in Mark Messier and Wayne Gretzky. Messier is both big and fast, with a 100-mph slapshot and a willingness to check. He is truly an all-around hockey player.

Messier was only 17 years old when he turned pro with the Indianapolis Racers of the old WHA in 1978. Edmonton selected him in the second round of the 1979 NHL draft, and Messier responded by scoring 33 points in his first season. He scored 63 in his second season. He soon became a consistent 50-goal per year player. With Gretzky and Messier leading the attack, the Oilers stole the Stanley Cup four times in five years. Messier's most productive season was 1989-90, when he scored 129 points on 45 goals and 84 assists, winning both the Hart Trophy as the league's MVP and the Stanley Cup for his team.

Edmonton traded Messier to the New York Rangers in 1990. In his first game in a Ranger uniform, Messier brought New York from behind to score a 2-1 overtime victory against Montreal. For his career, Messier has so far compiled 1,232 points (452 goals and 780 assists) in 1,005 regular-season games. Messier will surely end up near the top of many record lists.

The Great One

Perhaps no player has had a more profound impact on his sport than Wayne Gretzky has had on hockey. He has combined skill, determination, intelligence, and some magical sixth sense to fashion the most remarkable career ever. No hockey player, with the possible exception of Mario Lemieux, even comes close to Gretzky's level of consistent greatness.

Gretzky was a hockey prodigy, scoring goals with ease as a child. When he was ten years old he once scored nine goals in one game. By the time he was 17, he was the most eagerly awaited hockey player in modern history. He played just one year in the old WHA before joining Edmonton. In his first 79 NHL games, Gretzky had 51 goals and a league-best 86 assists for

137 points—good enough to tie Marcel Dionne for the best record in the league.

During the next 11 years (1980-91), Gretzky led the league in scoring nine times, won the Hart Trophy as the NHL's best player eight years in a row, and captained the Oilers to four Stanley Cup championships. In 1981-82, the Great One set all-time records for goals in a season with 92 and for assists with 120—65 total points better than Mike Bossy, his nearest competitor. During that stretch, Gretzky scored 50 goals in 39 games, faster than anyone else ever had.

Gretzky's many records and trophies could fill a book. There are so many ingredients to his success. He has great playmaking skill, and his stickhandling is without peer. He can steal a puck better than anyone else, and, when he has it, won't give it up. He possesses great stamina and can play 30 and 40 minutes per game. He changed the center position, and makes all of his teammates play better.

On October 15, 1989, Gretzky became the NHL's all-time leading scorer when he hit point number 1,851, surpassing Gordie Howe's mark. Gretzky showed no signs of slowing down as he scored his 2,000th career point in 1990-91, and led the league in scoring for the ninth time (163 points). Now playing for the L.A. Kings, Gretzky holds more than 50 hockey records. To put it simply, the Great One lives up to his nickname.

Mario Lemieux

If Wayne Gretzky is the greatest player in hockey history, Mario Lemieux is the greatest player of today. No one in the league can compare with this gifted man. The big center for the Pittsburgh Penguins became only the third rookie in NHL history to score 100 points (43 goals and 57 assists). In 1987-88 he surpassed Gretzky for the goal (70) and point (168) leadership in the NHL.

The center of the 1990s, and a sure Hall-of-Famer, is the Penguin's mighty Mario Lemieux.

In so doing he also won the Hart Trophy. The following year he stunned the league by threatening Gretzky's all-time season records when he scored 85 goals, 114 assists, and 199 points.

Even hampered by injuries, Lemieux led the Penguins to the Stanley Cup in 1990-91. The next year Lemieux did it again, taking the Penguins all the way to the Cup and his second Conn Smythe.

Lemieux's great size makes him an ideal center, and his remarkable talent makes him the deadliest scorer in the league today. He anticipates very well: "Before I get the puck, I watch where the players are and try to determine where they will be after," he says. "I try to get a crowd to go after me, then pass to whoever's open. It's easy." Maybe easy for him, but not for anyone else.

Lemieux has battled back from back injuries and even Hodgkin's Disease which have threatened his career. He just keeps on winning.

Most Points: Career

Name	Teams	Points	Yrs in NHL
Wayne Gretzky	Edmonton, L.A.	2,393	15
Gordie Howe	Detroit, Hartford	1,850	26
Marcel Dionne	Detroit, L.A., NY Rangers	1,771	18
Phil Esposito	Boston, NY Rangers	1,590	18
Stan Mikita	Chicago	1,467	23

Most Hart Trophies (League MVP)

Name	Teams	Trophies	Yrs in NHL
Wayne Gretzky	Edmonton, L.A.	9	15
Gordie Howe	Detroit	6	26
Eddie Shore	Boston	4	14
Howie Morenz	Montreal	3	14
Bobby Orr	Boston	3	12

Most Art Ross Trophies (Highest Season Scorer)

Name	Teams	Trophies	Yrs in NHL
Wayne Gretzky	Edmonton, L.A.	10	15
Gordie Howe	Detroit	5	26
Phil Esposito	Boston	5	18
Stan Mikita	Chicago	4	23
Mario Lemieux	Pittsburgh	3	9
Guy Lafleur	Montreal	3	17

Glossary

BODY CHECK. To use one's body to block an opponent. Legal only when the man hit has the puck or was the last player to have touched it.

BREAKAWAY. When a player has managed to get behind the opposing defense with the puck and is skating in all alone on the opposing goalie.

CHECKING. Defending against or guarding an opponent. On a line, a right wing checks the other team's left wing and a left wing check's the opposing right wing. Centers check each other.

CREASE. The area marked off in front of each net. Only a goalie is permitted in the crease, and no player may score from there unless he is being pinned in by a defending player.

DEKE. To feint or shift an opponent out of position.

PENALTY-KILLER. A player whose job is to stop the opposing team when his team is one or two men short after a penalty is called.

PLAYMAKER. Usually a center whose skating, puck-carrying, or passing abilities enable him to set up or make a play that can lead to a goal.

POWER PLAY. A manpower advantage resulting from a penalty to the opposing team.

SLAPSHOT. When a player winds up and slaps the puck with his stick, resulting in a hard, fast, but often erratic shot.

STICKHANDLING. The art of controlling the puck with the stick.

Bibliography

Diamond, Dan & Joseph Romain. *Hockey Hall of Fame.* New York: Doubleday, 1988.

Diamond, Dan, ed. *National Hockey League 75th Anniversary Commemorative Book.* Toronto, Canada: McClellan & Stewart, 1993.

Hollander, Zander, ed. *The Complete Encyclopedia of Hockey.* Detroit, MI: Visible Ink Press, 1993.

National Hockey League. *Official Guide & Record Book 1992-93.* Toronto, Canada: NHL Publications, 1993.

The Sporting News. *Sporting News Complete Hockey Book 1993-94.* St. Louis, MO: The Sporting News Publishing Co., 1993.

Photo Credits

Allsport: 14, 41 (Rick Stewart); 20 (Mike Powell); 22 (Harry Scull); 24, 33 (Ken Levine); 32, 40, 44; 34 (Gary Newkirk)

Hockey Hall of Fame: 4, 11 (Doug MacLellan); 9 (Imperial Oil/Turofsky); 10, 26, 30 (Frank Prazak); 17, 37

Index